What I Can Learn From The Incredible and Fantastic Life of Phil Knight
Published by Moppet Books
Los Angeles, California

Copyright © 2019 Moppet Books
All rights reserved including the right of reproduction in whole or in part in any form without written permission from the publisher.

ISBN: 978-0-9988205-9-0

Art direction and book design by Melissa Medina
Written by Fredrik Colting and Melissa Medina

Printed in China

www.moppetbookspublishing.com

What I Can Learn From The Incredible and Fantastic Life
— of —
Phil Knight

By Fredrik Colting & Melissa Medina
Illustrations By Natsuko Yoneyama

MOPPET BOOKS

Let's get to know Phil Knight.

He is a businessman and co-founder of Nike; you know, the shoe and sportswear company with the logo that looks like a ski slope. Phil's vision of a better shoe, or, as he called it, his "crazy idea," helped turn the sneaker into the most popular shoe in the entire world. Today, hundreds of millions of people wear them every day. Thanks, Phil!

Phil built more than just a cool shoe—he built an inspiring company. Nike was one of the first brands to make special shoes for famous athletes. This inspired a new generation to live healthy, dress comfortably, and do things their own way.

His dream of selling cool running shoes became one of the most iconic American brands in history.

Funtastic Facts
About Phil Knight

1. Phil's father owned a newspaper called The Oregon Journal, but he refused to give Phil a job. So Phil went to work for the competitor, The Oregonian, instead.

2. Phil was a good middle-distance runner and had a personal 1 mile best of 4 minutes and 10 seconds!

3. Phil co-founded the brand Nike with Bill Bowerman, who was his track coach at the University of Oregon.

4. Before it was called Nike, Phil named their shoe company "Blue Ribbon Sports."

5   The first sneakers sold by Phil were samples from a Japanese brand called Onitsuka that Bowerman made manual adjustments to.

6   Phil sold their first sneakers out of his car trunk at track meets.

7   Phil paid a student named Carolyn Davidson just $35 to design the famous Nike "swoosh" logo. Years later he gave her a diamond ring and $600,000 worth of Nike shares.

8   Phil thinks it's good to stand out. That's why he decided Nike's shoe boxes should be bright orange.

9   Phil has donated more than $2 billion dollars to different charities.

10   Phil bought an animation studio in 2011, which later made the hit movie *Coraline*.

Let's start from the very beginning...

Phil was born in Portland, Oregon, in 1938, and grew up with his parents and two sisters. He was kind of a shy kid, but he loved sports—especially baseball. Unfortunately, when he was 12, he was cut from the school team. He felt devastated. Phil hated feeling like he wasn't good enough, and if there was one thing Phil didn't like, it was losing.

To get his mind off things, he practiced high jump in the backyard. One day Phil's mom came running from out of nowhere and flew over the bar! She was a pretty cool mom and did it to cheer him up. She told him to forget about baseball and become a runner instead. "You're a fast boy," she said.

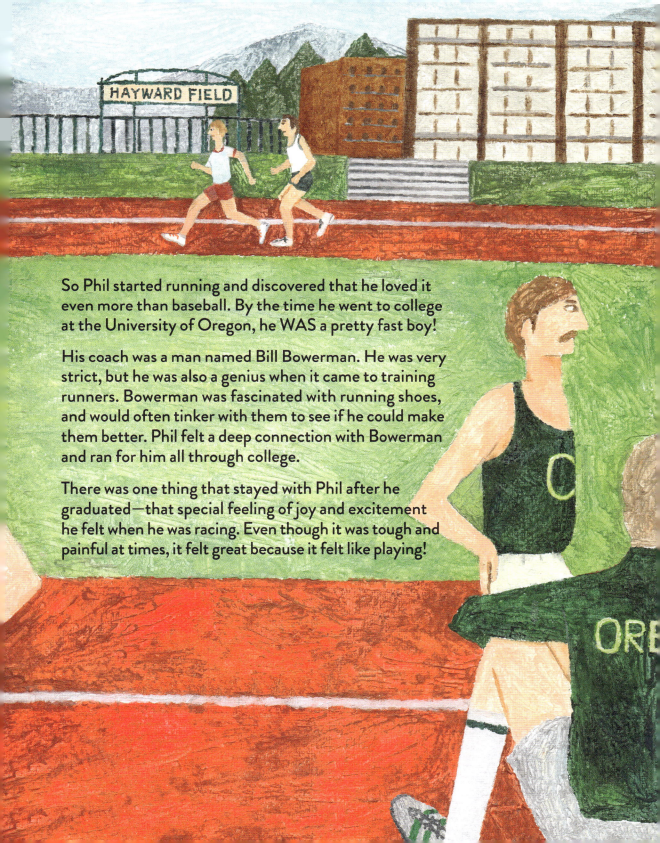

So Phil started running and discovered that he loved it even more than baseball. By the time he went to college at the University of Oregon, he WAS a pretty fast boy!

His coach was a man named Bill Bowerman. He was very strict, but he was also a genius when it came to training runners. Bowerman was fascinated with running shoes, and would often tinker with them to see if he could make them better. Phil felt a deep connection with Bowerman and ran for him all through college.

There was one thing that stayed with Phil after he graduated—that special feeling of joy and excitement he felt when he was racing. Even though it was tough and painful at times, it felt great because it felt like playing!

Phil studied journalism in college, but after graduation he wasn't sure that's what he really wanted to do. While waiting for his dreams to become clear, he spent a year in the Army, then decided to study business at Stanford University where he learned the meaning of the word "entrepreneur"—

Someone who is a risk-taker and wants to start their own business. That's me! Phil thought.

In that same class he wrote a paper on a new type of Japanese sports shoes called Onitsuka Tiger, and even though he hadn't thought much about shoes before, something about it grabbed him.

After Stanford, Phil moved back to Oregon, still not sure what he wanted to do with his life. The one thing that always helped him think was running. So he put his sneakers on and headed out into the Oregon forest. Soon his legs and breath moved automatically, and his mind was free to think. Phil knew he wanted to do something different. He wanted people to remember him for something good. As he kept running suddenly it was just there, Phil's crazy idea: What if he could start a company that sold the best sports shoes in the world? Just like those Japanese shoes. Then he could work with something he loved while helping other athletes. Yes, this was his dream!

Now that Phil knew what he wanted to do with his life, he couldn't wait to get started! The first thing he did was borrow some money to go to Japan. There he wandered through streets that were still in ruin from World War II and visited many Zen temples. Zen is a way of thinking and viewing life where there is no future or past, only right now, which was sort of the same feeling Phil got from running—the feeling that nothing else existed.

He went to visit the Onitsuka Tiger factory and fell in love with their shoes so much that he asked to become their distributor in the US. It was a bit of a stretch because Phil didn't even have a company yet. So he pretended that he did. When asked about it all he could think of were the blue ribbons he got for running track back in Oregon. "The name of my company is...Blue Ribbon Sports," he told them. Everyone thought it sounded pretty official, so they gave him the deal to distribute their shoes.

Phil returned back to Oregon and soon received a box of shoes from the factory in Japan. He immediately gave a pair to his old coach, Bill Bowerman, who was so impressed that he said he wanted to partner with Phil in his new shoe company. Together they officially founded Blue Ribbon Sports in 1964.

While Bowerman worked on making the shoes better, Phil was in charge of sales. They didn't have a store, so Phil drove around to different track meets and sold the sneakers out of the trunk of his car. He didn't think he would be a very good salesman, but he was wrong. He quickly sold all the shoes, and realized that because he really *loved* what he was selling, it made all the difference in the world!

The rumor about Phil's cool new lightweight sneakers spread and soon people were even showing up at his house to buy them. Phil realized he needed a real store, so they opened the first Blue Ribbon Sports store in Santa Monica, California, in 1966. They hired employees, and things were going really well.

BLUE RIBBON SPORTS GRAND OPENING!

PHIL'S DREAM WAS BECOMING A REALITY!

He fell in love with a woman named Penelope, and in 1968 they got married. Life was going his way and Phil couldn't have been happier!

However, life then decided to throw him a real curve ball. Out of nowhere, the Onitsuko Tiger factory in Japan told him they wouldn't give him any more shoes. Then the bank told him they wouldn't loan him any more money. Phil's dream was crumbling before his eyes.

Phil thought back to what Bowerman taught him about running. Even when it is hard, you never give up! So he came up with a plan. He gathered all their employees and told them that this was the moment to create their own destiny. He told them they would start making their own shoes! Only one thing was missing. What should they call their new company? One employee suggested the name Nike, which is the name of the winged Greek goddess of victory. That's perfect!, Phil thought.

It was a hectic time for Phil and everyone at Nike. Bowerman kept experimenting with the shoes and even used his wife's waffle iron to come up with a new type of sole he called the waffle sole!

Finally, in 1972, they were ready to present the first original Nike shoes to the world. Phil was really nervous. What if his dream was just a crazy idea? But it turned out he didn't have to worry, because everybody wanted a pair of Nikes!

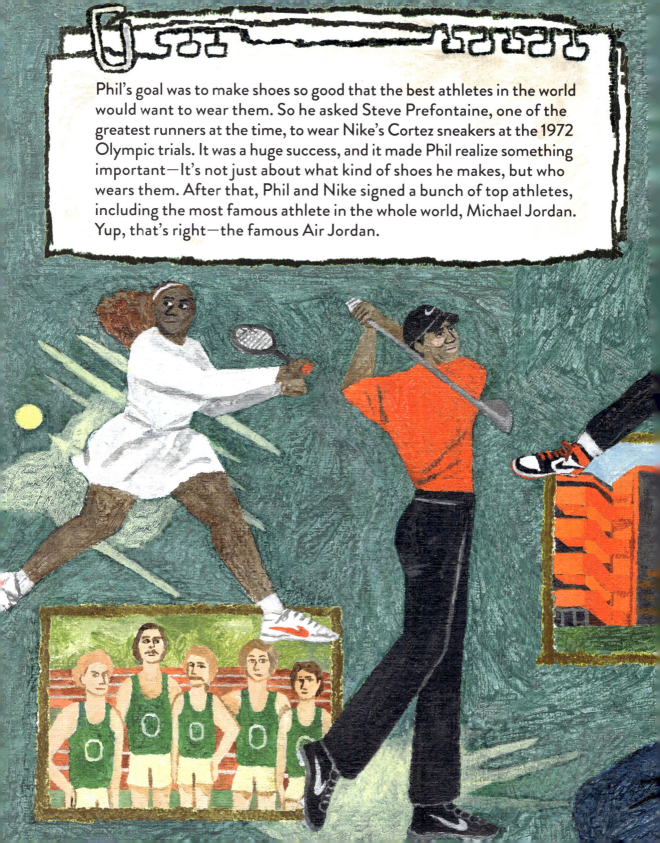

Phil's goal was to make shoes so good that the best athletes in the world would want to wear them. So he asked Steve Prefontaine, one of the greatest runners at the time, to wear Nike's Cortez sneakers at the 1972 Olympic trials. It was a huge success, and it made Phil realize something important—It's not just about what kind of shoes he makes, but who wears them. After that, Phil and Nike signed a bunch of top athletes, including the most famous athlete in the whole world, Michael Jordan. Yup, that's right—the famous Air Jordan.

After this, Nike quickly grew bigger, year after year. There were some ups and downs, but Phil dealt with it all the same way—by never giving up and believing in his dream. Today Nike is the biggest athletic shoe and clothing company in the world, and Phil has inspired millions of adults and kids to become athletes, stay active, and, you know...just do it!

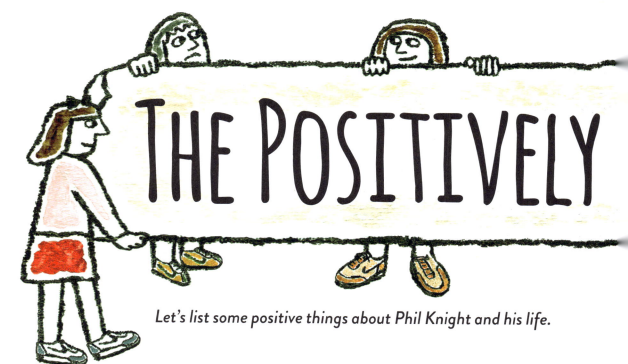

THE POSITIVELY

Let's list some positive things about Phil Knight and his life.

Phil inspires us

People can inspire us in different ways. Phil's company inspires lots of people to be active and enjoy sports and exercise. And everybody knows that being active is important for both health and happiness.

Phil believes in his dreams

Believing in your dreams inspires other people to believe in theirs. Sometimes it takes people like Phil to remind us that our dreams, even if they seem crazy, can make a difference.

Positive List

Phil is a good role model

Phil's hard work has paid off and he's become very wealthy. But he doesn't keep all that money to himself. He donates millions of dollars to different charities and tries to use his success to help other people succeed. That's called Philanthropy (it's not named after Phil, even though it does sound like it).

Phil cares about the environment

Making shoes can create a lot of waste, especially for a big company like Nike, but Phil insists they try to use as much renewable energy and recycled materials as possible.

How Can I Be Great Like Phil Knight?

First of all, you should always be yourself because you are already great! But it is a good idea to learn from people that have experience. Here are a few great things we can learn from Phil.

TRUST your DREAMS!

Everybody has dreams. Small ones, big ones, medium ones. Sometimes when we tell other people about them they will say our dreams are wrong, or even stupid. But you should believe in your own dreams regardless of what other people think. If it's important to YOU, that's what matters!

GO FOR A RUN!

When you are thinking hard about something, trying to come up with a solution for a problem, it can really help if you go for a run. Or jump on a trampoline, or swim, or ride your bike—anything that makes you move, helps you think!

Just Do it!

We all make mistakes, it's just part of life—but who says mistakes are always bad? Most mistakes can actually be good because we learn from them. If we don't make mistakes that means we aren't even trying. So get out there and just do it!

BIBLIOGRAPHY

Martin, Emmie, "How Phil Knight Built Nike...," Businessinsider.com, Accessed March 12, 2018.

Knight, Phil, "Shoe Dog," Simon & Schuster, 2016.

Golden, Jessica, "How Phil Knight turned a dream into a $25 billion fortune" cnbc.com, May 9, 2016.

Bennett, Donnovan, "My Work of Art is Nike," sportsnet.ca.

Fisk, Peter, "Phil Knight's Fantastic History of Nike...," thegeniusworks.com, August 21, 2018.

Biography.yourdictionary.com, "Phil Knight," Accessed January 1, 2018.

Wikipedia.com, "Phil Knight," Accessed February 15, 2018.